First World War
and Army of Occupation
War Diary
France, Belgium and Germany

17 DIVISION
51 Infantry Brigade,
Brigade Trench Mortar Battery
10 November 1915 - 31 January 1916

WO95/2008/4

The Naval & Military Press Ltd
www.nmarchive.com
Published in association with The National Archives

Published by

The Naval & Military Press Ltd

Unit 10 Ridgewood Industrial Park,

Uckfield, East Sussex,

TN22 5QE England

Tel: +44 (0) 1825 749494

www.naval-military-press.com

www.nmarchive.com

This diary has been reprinted in facsimile from the original. Any imperfections are inevitably reproduced and the quality may fall short of modern type and cartographic standards.

© **Crown Copyright**
Images reproduced by permission of The National Archives, London, England, 2015.

Contents

Document type	Place/Title	Date From	Date To
Heading	51 Infantry Brigade Brigade Trench Mortar Battery. 1915 Nov-1916 Jan		
Heading	17 Div 51 Bde 51 Trench Mortar Bty 1915 Nov To 1916 Jan		
War Diary		10/11/1915	14/11/1915
War Diary	Centre Sector 21st-Div	15/11/1915	21/11/1915
War Diary	21st Div	22/11/1915	31/12/1915
Miscellaneous	51/46 Trench Mortar Bty Jan 1916 Vol III		
War Diary	Sheet 36 c 28 d 7-1	01/01/1916	31/01/1916

2008/14

51 Infantry Brigade

Brigade Trench Mortar Battery.

1915 Nov – 1916 Jan

~~2 ARMY TROOPS~~

17 DIV. 51 Bde

51

TRENCH MORTAR

BTY

1915 NOV TO 1916 JAN

(1725)

Army Form. C. 2118

WAR DIARY
or
INTELLIGENCE SUMMARY 51st Bty, Trench Mortars R.G.A
(Erase heading not required.)

Instructions regarding War Diaries and Intelligence Summaries are contained in F. S. Regs., Part II. and the Staff Manual respectively. Title Pages will be prepared in manuscript.

Place	Date	Hour	Summary of Events and Information	Remarks and references to Appendices
	1915 Nov 10th	—	Battery formed at Brigade Hd Quarters — less one Officer. Lieut A. Ibbitson R.F.A. Commanding — 11 R.G.A. and 1/2 K.O.Y.L.I. (9th Battn) other ranks. Armed with four 2" mortars complete and four spare ones.	
	12th	—	Joined 21st Div.	
	13th	—	Visited Right and Centre Sectors of Div: front and selected, after reconnoitring Emp: of hostile trenches, two positions for mortar emplacements.	
	14th	—	Commenced digging in mortar emplacement, dug-outs for personnel, store for bombs. "th funk pit" with	

A W Ibbitson Lt RFA

Army Form. C. 2118

WAR DIARY
or
INTELLIGENCE SUMMARY

(Erase heading not required.)

51 T.M. Battery

Instructions regarding War Diaries and Intelligence Summaries are contained in F. S. Regs., Part II. and the Staff Manual respectively. Title Pages will be prepared in manuscript.

Place	Date	Hour	Summary of Events and Information	Remarks and references to Appendices
Centre Section 51st Div	Nov 15		Digging etc — providing Emplacements, Dugouts & Bombstores.	
	16		— do — — do — Fired actual round—blind.	2 in.
	17		— do — — do —. Fired 4 rounds (2") all "blind".	
	18		— do — — do — — do — Fired 3 rounds, 1 blind 2 good. The good ones were obtained by firing with full charge, this charge apparently being the only one that will function the fuze. The target in all above instances was German trench salient at 220 yards. Lt W.H.Robertson joined	
	19 20 21		Digging etc same as on previous day/s Handed over a 2" gun to each of 42 & 4/5th Batts. Took over six guns 1½" 4" 4lb 4lb/bars from 23rd Bty $\frac{1}{2} \frac{4}{2} \frac{4}{1}$	

W.R. 23/11

W.Robertson Lt. R.F.A.
comdg 51st T.M.Bty.

Army Form. C. 2118

WAR DIARY
or
INTELLIGENCE SUMMARY
(Erase heading not required.)

51st Trench Mortar Battery

Instructions regarding War Diaries and Intelligence Summaries are contained in F. S. Regs., Part II. and the Staff Manual respectively. Title Pages will be prepared in manuscript.

Place	Date Nov.	Hour	Summary of Events and Information	Remarks and references to Appendices
21st Div.	22		Digging Emplacements & building up.	
	23		do	
	24		do	
	25		Fired into enemy trenches opposite "74" – eight 4" shell – all good. " " " " " "80" – three " – two " – 1 blind Digging Emplacements building up	
	26		do	

			Fired a 2" bomb at SPARROWS NEST – blind } for
			  " " " " " " . Trench opposite "74" – Good } Registration
			  " " two 4 lb bombs at Trench opposite 76 – 1 blind, 1 good
			Digging & building emplacements.	

	27		Digging & building emplacements. Fired an 18 lb bomb at farm "73" – Blind (to resistance)	
	28		Digging and building Emplacements.	

A Hobson Lt RFA.

Army Form. C. 2118

WAR DIARY
or
INTELLIGENCE SUMMARY

(Erase heading not required.)

51ˢᵗ Trench Mortar Battery

Instructions regarding War Diaries and Intelligence Summaries are contained in F. S. Regs., Part II. and the Staff Manual respectively. Title Pages will be prepared in manuscript.

Place	Date	Hour	Summary of Events and Information	Remarks and references to Appendices
21ˢᵗ Div.	Nov. 29		Digging and building Emplacements.	
	30		do —	
	Dec 1		do —	
	2		do —	
	3		do —	
	4		Fired into enemy's Trenches at Farm A, opposite 78 Trench, eleven 2" shells — all good	
			" " Farm B, opposite 79 Trench five 2" shells — all good	
			The above was in cooperation with the artillery and infantry. The shooting was good as far as could be judged in the darkness. The enemy retaliated but no shells fell within forty yards of our emplacements. E.M.D.	
	5		Digging and building Emplacements	

W.Y. Robertson 2ⁿᵈ Lt 3. Com. Royal
F.C. 57ᵗʰ D.M. Battery

Army Form C 2118

WAR DIARY
or
INTELLIGENCE SUMMARY
(Erase heading not required.) 5/1 Trench Mortar Battery

Instructions regarding War Diaries and Intelligence Summaries are contained in F. S. Regs., Part II. and the Staff Manual respectively. Title Pages will be prepared in manuscript.

Place	Date	Hour	Summary of Events and Information	Remarks and references to Appendices
21st Div.	Dec. 6		Digging and building emplacements.	
	7		Digging emplacements and drying dugouts.	
	8.		Fired 15 rounds from 2" gun in no 74 Trench. 13 were good but 2 were "shorts". The target was Sparrow's nest from which we succeeded in damaging to a considerable content. The enemy made no attempt to retaliate either during or after firing.	
	9		Digging emplacements and improving dugouts.	
	10		Improving gun beds and covering emplacements to hide them.	
	11.		Digging and building emplacements.	
	12			

W.Y. Robertson 2 Lt 3 Coy Ray

Army Form. C. 2118

WAR DIARY
or
INTELLIGENCE SUMMARY

(Erase heading not required.)

51st Trench Mortar Battery

Instructions regarding War Diaries and Intelligence Summaries are contained in F. S. Regs., Part II. and the Staff Manual respectively. Title Pages will be prepared in manuscript.

Place	Date	Hour	Summary of Events and Information	Remarks and references to Appendices
	Dec 12th	—	Building emplacements and improving gun pits	WD/1/15
	Dec 13th	—	ditto	
	Dec 14th	—	S.A.A. transferred one 2" gun and one four pounder gun to 42nd Battery for use in the 15/16 Div.	
	Dec 15th	—	Building emplacements. Sent 4.2" Battery three men for scheme on 17th 15/15	
	Dec 16th	—	Building emplacements. Guns and men returned. At request of an infantry officer fired three rounds from a 1.5" gun at a German working party. All three were dumb. They were fitted with the old type of fuze.	
	Dec 17th	—	Started new defensive emplacement but work was very difficult owing to water.	
	Dec 18th	—	Building emplacements and improving dug-outs	

W. G. Robertson Capt
Comdg 51st Trench M. Battery

Army Form. C. 2118

WAR DIARY
or
INTELLIGENCE SUMMARY 51st Trench Mortar Battery
(Erase heading not required.)

Instructions regarding War Diaries and Intelligence Summaries are contained in F. S. Regs., Part II. and the Staff Manual respectively. Title Pages will be prepared in manuscript.

Place	Date	Hour	Summary of Events and Information	Remarks and references to Appendices
	Dec 19th		Building emplacements and improving gun pits	
	Dec 20th		Battery fired two 2" bombs at German trenches opposite the Ghoull Salient to silence the German rifle grenades. The firing (especially connectivity)	
	Dec 21st		Fired four (4) 2" bombs from gun emplacement at ISA3.3 all were blinds. The ammunition used had been salved from a flooded bombstore and taken over from the 50th Division but is still too damp to use.	
			Fired five 2" bombs from emplacement at ISC4.3 at Sharran's Nest Farm. All were good and did considerable damage to the farm. The enemy made no attempt to retaliate.	
	Dec 22nd		Fired four 2" bombs from gun emplacement at ISA3.3 at Farm A. Three were good and registered direct hit on the farm. One was a blind. The enemy retaliated but failed to find our position.	
	Dec 23rd		Building new defensive emplacement.	
	Dec 24th		Sitt	
	Dec 25th		Sitt	

W. Y. Robertson 2/Lt
Comdg 51st Trench Mortar Battery

Army Form. C. 2118

WAR DIARY
or
INTELLIGENCE SUMMARY 51st Trench Mortar Battery 3/7
(Erase heading not required.)

Instructions regarding War Diaries and Intelligence Summaries are contained in F. S. Regs., Part II. and the Staff Manual respectively. Title Pages will be prepared in manuscript.

Place	Date	Hour	Summary of Events and Information	Remarks and references to Appendices
	Dec 26th		Abandoned old defensive position for gun emplacement owing to state of ground and selected new position. Transferred one 2" gun to 25th Division for action on 27th.	
	27th		Started new defensive emplacement.	
	28th		Working on defensive emplacement. Gun returned by 25th Division.	
	29th		ditto	
	30th		ditto	
	31st		ditto	

W. H. Robertson 2 Lt.
Comdg. 51st Trench Mortar Battery

51/46 Trench Mortar Bty
Jan 1916
Vol III

Army Form C. 2118.

WAR DIARY
or
INTELLIGENCE SUMMARY
(Erase heading not required).

51st Trench Mortar Bty

Instructions regarding War Diaries and Intelligence Summaries are contained in F. S. Regs., Part II, and the Staff Manual respectively. Title Pages will be prepared in manuscript.

Place	Date	Hour	Summary of Events and Information	Remarks and references to Appendices
Sheet 36 C.28.D.7.1.	1st		Am taking emplacement and endeavouring to complete old ones.	
	2nd		One defensive emplacement completed. Started work on dugout and bomb store.	
	3rd		Second defensive emplacement started	
	4th		Working on emplacements and clearing guns	
	5th		nil	
	6th	20p.	Fired thirty 2" bombs & 20 1½" light bombs. The target was Fort Ballot Salient (C.29.a.3½.1½). There were two rounds with the 1½" bombs but all the 2" bombs detonated. The 2" bombs burst bombs-nests into the air but what will be seen to any considerable extent the 1½" bombs do not appear to any considerable extent the 1½" bombs there was a little retaliation but no damage was done. Chinking emplacements and re-laying gun beds.	

W.H. Robertson 2/Lt

WAR DIARY or INTELLIGENCE SUMMARY

Army Form C. 2118.

59th Trench Mortar Battery

Place	Date	Hour	Summary of Events and Information	Remarks and references to Appendices
Neuve 36 C.36.d.7.1	1917 Jan 8th		Improving emplacements and communications to gun positions	
	9th		Ditto —	
	10th		Ditto — Built temporary emplacement for action on Jan 11th	
	11th	11:30A	Fired 21 2" bombs of which one was a "three" and 25 1½" bombs (2 blinds) and 20 4lb bombs. The target was Fort Ballot Salient (C.29.a.3½.1½). The damage to the enemy wire was very considerable and the parapet was breached.	
		11:15p	On the night of the 11th size 2" bombs were fired and 25 4lb bombs. All detonated well but observation was impossible owing to the darkness. There was considerable shattering part of the protection of the 2" gun position.	
	12th		Cleaning emplacements and relaying gun beds.	
	13th		Overhauling all the emplacements and improving same	
	14th		Ditto —	

Lt A Robertson 2Lt
for O.C. 59th Tr. Mr. Batty.

Army Form. C. 2118

WAR DIARY
or
INTELLIGENCE SUMMARY

5th Trench Mortar Battery

(Erase heading not required.)

Instructions regarding War Diaries and Intelligence Summaries are contained in F. S. Regs., Part II. and the Staff Manual respectively. Title Pages will be prepared in manuscript.

Place	Date	Hour	Summary of Events and Information	Remarks and references to Appendices
No 12C Esd 7 1	Jan 15th		Started new emplacement and rebuilt one that had been struck by a shell	
	16th		Improving all emplacements	
	17th		Ditto —	
	18th		Ditto —	
	19th		Rebuilt communications to gun positions which had been damaged by shell fire	
	20th		Improving 6" emplacement and laying new trench	
	21st		Made arrangements to retaliate to German rifle grenades but was not called on to do so.	
	22nd		Rebuilding overhead cover to three emplacements	

W. J. Robertson 2/Lt
for O.C. 5th T.M. Bty.

Army Form. C. 2118

WAR DIARY
or
INTELLIGENCE SUMMARY
(Erase heading not required.)

51st French Mortar Battery

Instructions regarding War Diaries and Intelligence Summaries are contained in F.S. Regs., Part II. and the Staff Manual respectively. Title Pages will be prepared in manuscript.

Place	Date	Hour	Summary of Events and Information	Remarks and references to Appendices
Sh L 3.6	23rd June		Preparing three emplacements for action on 24th	
C28 d 7.1	24th	11:30 A	Fired 15 2" bombs, 6 light 1½" bombs, 14 heavy 1½" bombs and 2 D/4 lb bombs at Fort Balliol salient (C 29 35, 15). All detonated well and after one 2" bomb had exploded in the German trenches, another explosion was seen to take place, much debris being thrown in the air. A similar explosion took place after one of the 4 lb bombs had exploded. After the fifteenth round from the 2" gun, the enemy hit the emplacement to, killing three men and wrecking one and destroying the gun.	
	25th		Cleaning up emplacements.	
	26th		Cleaning guns and tools and working on defensive emplacements.	
	27th		Ditto	
	28th		Ditto	
	29th		Started work on two new emplacements	
	30th		Ditto	
	31st		Ditto	

W. Y. Robertson 2/Lt
for O.C. 51st Fr. Mr. Batty.

www.ingramcontent.com/pod-product-compliance
Lightning Source LLC
Chambersburg PA
CBHW081511160426
43193CB00014B/2653